Draw Your Own Encyclopaedia
Space Exploration
Classroom Edition

Colin M. Drysdale

Pictish Beast Publications

Text Copyright © 2019 Colin M. Drysdale
Imprint and Layout Copyright © 2019 Colin M. Drysdale /Pictish Beast Publications

All rights reserved.
This is the classroom edition of *Draw Your Own Encyclopaedia Space Exploration*. This means that the cost of this book includes the right to photocopy its contents to produce handouts for use in classrooms and for other educational purposes. However, they cannot be reproduced for any 'for-profit' activity without express permission.

ISBN - 978-1-909832-67-1
Published by Pictish Beast Publications, Glasgow, UK.
Published in the United Kingdom
First Printing: 2019. First Edition.

A non-classroom edition of this book for individual children is also available (ISBN: 978-1-909832-49-7).

The cover image is copyright © Vadim Sadovskir/Shutterstock.com

www.PictishBeastPublications.com

Introduction

This book is part of the *Draw Your Own Encyclopaedia* series of factual books for children aged six to twelve. It provides interesting introductions to a variety of different areas related to space exploration. This classroom edition is aimed at teachers and other educators (rather than at individual children, as is the case for the individual edition). It contains:

- Eleven double-page spreads which explore a range of topics about space exploration that can be photocopied to create handouts for use in the classroom or as homework assignments. Each one contains an introductory question, a paragraph that explores its topic, questions to test your students comprehension of the contents of this paragraph, quick facts to provide additional information, and space for the student to add their own illustration for this topic.

- A blank *Draw Your Own Encyclopaedia* double-page spread which you can photocopy and hand out to your students to allow them to create their own custom encyclopaedia entry based on a topic related to space exploration of their (or your) choice.

- Two handouts which you can use to introduce mathematics into your lessons about space exploration. The first allows your students to work out how much food they would need to grow to support a colony on Mars, while the second allows them to calculate how long it would take a spacecraft to reach each of the other planets in our solar system.

- A sixteen-question pop quiz that you can use to test your students knowledge about space exploration. All the information needed to answer these questions is contained in this book.

- Links to additional background information about space exploration which you can use to increase your own knowledge of this subject.

- Links to free online content, such as videos, related to the topics covered in this book that you can show to your students.

- Ideas for six interactive and fun additional classroom activities.

Thus, taken together, the contents of this book provide you with all the information you need to teach your class all about space exploration in a fun and interesting way that integrates factual knowledge, reading comprehension, maths skills and practical demonstrations.

Who Was The First Person In Space?

The first person ever to visit space was called Uri Gagarin. He was a Russian cosmonaut, and he was blasted into space on the top of a very powerful rocket on the 12th of April 1961. It was an incredibly dangerous journey, and as he was the first person to do it, no one knew if he would survive the trip. Luckily, he did. His space capsule, called Vostok 1, spent one hour and forty-eight minutes in space, which was enough time for him to complete a single orbit of the Earth. Since this first ever space flight, hundreds of people (both men and women) have travelled into space.

Quick Fact: While Uri Gagarin was the first person in space, he was not the first living thing to go into space. Instead, this honour goes to a dog called Laika. She was launched into space by the Russians in November 1957 as a way of test the technology that would later be used by Uri Gagarin for the first ever human space flight.

Questions To Answer:

1. Who was the first person in space?

2. What was the name of his space capsule?

3. How long did he spend in space?

From *Draw Your Own Encyclopaedia Space Exploration* by Colin M. Drysdale

Quick Fact: The first man-made object sent into space was a satellite called Sputnik 1. It was launched in October 1957 and spent almost three months circling the Earth.

Quick Fact: While the Russians call their space explorers cosmonauts, those who fly on American spacecraft are called astronauts.

The Vostok 1 space capsule was little more than a large metal ball with just enough room for Uri Gagarin to lie down in it. Draw a picture of him lying down in his Vostok 1 space capsule as he orbited the Earth for the first time.

How Do Rockets Work?

Since the first space flights in the 1950s and 1960s, rockets have been used to blast spacecraft into space. While they may seem very complicated, a rocket engine is very simple. It is just a narrow neck fitted on to a tube, and it has no moving parts. Its power comes from a chemical reaction between two parts of the rocket fuel. When mixed together, these parts undergo an exothermic chemical reaction that generates heat and gases. With nowhere else to go, these gases are forced out through the narrow neck and propel the rocket upwards. This allows the rocket to reach speeds of more than 40,000 kilometres an hour, which is the speed needed to overcome the Earth's gravity and reach space.

Questions To Answer:

1. How many moving parts does a rocket engine have?

2. What type of chemical reaction powers a rocket?

3. How fast does a rocket need to go to reach space?

From *Draw Your Own Encyclopaedia Space Exploration* by Colin M. Drysdale

The space shuttle was the world's first re-usable spacecraft. However, in order to get it into space, it needed two external booster rockets and a very large fuel tank. Once the space shuttle was going fast enough, these would detach and fall back to Earth. Draw a picture of the space shuttle using its booster rockets to blast it into space.

When Did People First Land On The Moon?

The moon is the only place in our solar system, other than Earth, that people have visited. The first person to set foot on the moon was an American astronaut called Neil Armstrong. In 1969, it took Neil Armstrong and two colleagues just over three days to reach the moon, and no one was quite sure what they'd find when they got there. He, and a colleague called Buzz Aldrin, spent just over twenty-one hours on the moon before starting their journey back to the Earth. Since then, a total of twelve people, all Americans, have visited the moon.

Quick Fact: Since the moon has no atmosphere, it has no wind to disturb the dust on its surface. This means that Neil Armstrong's footprints (and the footprints of all the other astronauts who have walked there) will be visible for as long as the moon continues to exist.

Questions To Answer:

1. When did people first land on the moon?

2. What was the name of the first person to set foot on it?

3. How many people have walked on the moon?

Quick Fact: The astronauts that have visited the moon not only walked there, some of them also drove on the moon in a specially-built car called a moon buggy. This car is still on the moon, and it is proof that humans once visited another place in our solar system.

Since it has no atmosphere, humans can only survive on the moon if they wear specially-designed space suits. Each space suit has its own air supply to ensure that the astronaut has enough oxygen to breath. Draw a picture of an astronaut in a space suit walking on the moon.

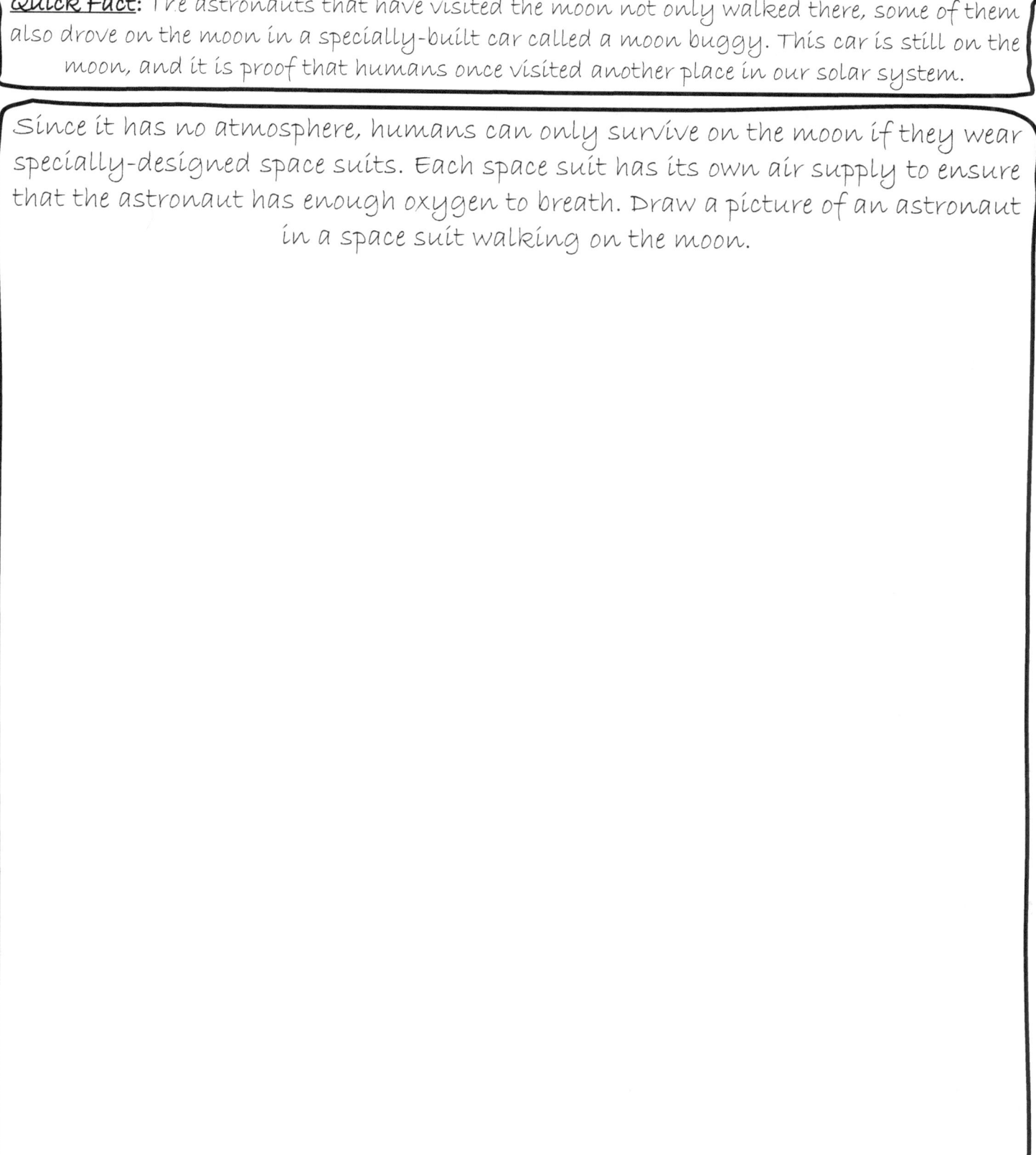

Quick Fact: As well as leaving behind their footprints and their moon buggy, astronauts also left behind some reflectors. These were positioned in such a way that people on Earth can fire a laser at them and bounce it back to Earth to accurately measure how far away the moon is. Anyone with the right kind of laser can do this, and it is further proof that humans once visited the moon.

How Do We Know What Other Planets Look Like?

While we can see other planets using telescopes, the best way to find out what they look like is to send a probe to visit them. A probe is an unmanned spacecraft fitted with lots of cameras and other scientific equipment. They can be sent to other planets to photograph them and study what they are made of. It can take a probe many years to reach another planet. For example, the Galileo spacecraft was launched in October 1989, but it did not reach Jupiter, its intended destination, until December 1995!

Quick Fact: We have not only sent probes to visit every planet in our solar system to learn more about them, we have also sent probes to study a number of their moons. We have even sent probes to study large asteroids and passing comets.

Quick Fact: It is not easy to change the route a probe will take once it has been launched. This means that successfully landing a probe on another planet is like throwing basket ball into a hoop that is ten miles away.

Questions To Answer:

1. What is a probe?

2. How long did it take the Galileo spacecraft to reach Jupiter?

From *Draw Your Own Encyclopaedia Space Exploration* by Colin M. Drysdale

Quick Fact: Probes send data back to Earth using radio signals. These can take a very long time to reach us, and they can only carry a little bit of information at a time. This means that it can take many months for a probe to send the data it collects back to Earth so that scientists can analyse it and work out what it shows.

The Mars Phoenix Lander was a probe designed to study whether Mars could support life (known as habitability). It weighed over 350 kilograms and was powered by solar panels. Draw a picture of this probe sitting on the surface of Mars, collecting data to send back to Earth.

Quick Fact: The information collected by probes has helped us find ice on Mars, oceans of methane on Europa and study the great red spot on Jupiter. However, as yet, no probe has detected any evidence of life anywhere else in our solar system, other than on Earth.

Are Robots Used To Explore Other Planets?

While most probes only orbit another planet, robotic probes can be used to explore their surface. Robotic probes capable of moving around are known as rovers. The very first rover to explore another planet was called Sojourner, and it undertook a journey of just 100 metres when it landed on Mars in 1997. Since then, more complex rovers have been used to explore Mars in much more detail. For example, the Opportunity rover landed on Mars in 2004. During its fourteen year life time, it travelled more than forty-five kilometres as it explored the Martian surface.

Questions To Answer:

1. What are robotic probes capable of moving around called?

2. When did the first rover land on Mars?

3. How far did the Opportunity rover travel on Mars?

From Draw Your Own Encyclopaedia Space Exploration by Colin M. Drysdale

The Opportunity rover was a six-wheeled robot that was 1.6 metres long, 1.5 metres high and weighed 185 kilograms. It was powered by batteries which were recharged using solar panels, and had a maximum speed of 0.18 kilometres an hour. Draw a picture of Opportunity exploring Mars here.

Quick Fact: The Opportunity rover mission was originally intended to last just ninety days. In the end, it lasted over 5,000! It's mission finally came to an end when a storm covered its solar panels with dust, meaning it could no longer recharge its batteries.

What Is The Furthest Distance Any Spacecraft Has Travelled?

While most spacecraft are sent to a specific destination, such as the moon or another planet, two spacecraft launched in 1977 were specifically sent off to explore the space beyond our solar system. These were the Voyager I and Voyager II spacecraft. So far, Voyager I has travelled over twenty billion kilometres. This is 145 times the distance between the Earth and the Sun. This is the furthest distance ever travelled by any man-made object. However, it will take a further 40,000 years to reach Proxima Centauri, our nearest neighbouring star system.

Questions To Answer:

1. When were the Voyager spacecraft launched?

2. How far has Voyager I travelled so far?

3. How long will it take Voyager I to reach our nearest neighbouring star system?

Each of the Voyager spacecraft carries a golden disc which contains information that will tell any aliens that find it what life is like on Earth. If you were asked to draw a single picture to be put on a spacecraft to tell aliens all about life on Earth, what would you draw? Draw your picture here.

Quick Fact: The Voyager I spacecraft is now so far from Earth that, even though they travel at the speed of light, it takes the radio signals it sends back over nineteen hours to reach us.

Does Anyone Live In Space?

The surprising answer to this question is yes. Since the year 2000, there have always been between three and six people living on the International Space Station or ISS. However, individual astronauts typically only spend about six months living on it. The ISS is the biggest object that we have ever put into space. It is 109 metres by 73 metres in size (which is slightly bigger than a football pitch). However, the main living space it only about 74 metres long, which is the same size as the inside of one and a half jumbo jet aeroplanes. Here, the crew must eat, sleep, work, relax, and go to the toilet.

Questions To Answer:

1. When was the International Space Station first occupied?

2. How big is the International Space Station?

3. How big are its living quarters?

From *Draw Your Own Encyclopaedia Space Exploration* by Colin M. Drysdale

The International Space Station (ISS) is 400 kilometres above the Earth, and it travels at a speed of 27,600 kilometres per hour. Despite it being so far away, if you look very carefully in the right place at the right time, you can see the ISS as it flies overhead. Draw a picture of the ISS here.

Quick Fact: The International Space Station orbits the Earth every 92 minutes. This means that the people who live on it sees around fifteen sunrises each day!

Quick Fact: It costs a lot of money to transport supplies to the ISS. This means that the crew must recycle as much stuff as they possibly can. This includes recycling water from condensation that collects on the inside (which comes from sweat and exhaled breath), from shower water, and even from urine! While this sounds pretty awful, once it has been purified and filtered, it is no different from the water that comes out of your taps at home.

How Could We Set Up A Colony On Mars?

Setting up a colony on Mars would be possible, but it wouldn't be easy. Since Mars does not have a breathable atmosphere, the first thing that any colonists would need to do would be to build structures for them to live in. Once these structures have been built, the colonists would need a way to produce oxygen to breathe, water to drink, food to eat and power. Luckily, power can be generated using solar panels, and this can be used to melt Martian ice to produce water. Electricity from solar panels can also be used to break water down into oxygen to breath, and hydrogen, which can be used as a fuel.

Questions To Answer:

1. What is the first thing that colonists would need to do to be able to live on Mars?

2. How could Mars colonists generate power?

3. Where could Mars colonists get water from?

Draw a picture of what you think a colony on Mars would look like, and add labels to show where the colonists would sleep, eat, exercise, grow their own food, get water from and generate their power.

Quick Fact: In order to grow food on Mars, the colonists would need a good quality fertiliser. It would be too expensive and difficult to bring this from Earth, so they would need to find another source. Luckily, there is something that all humans produce on a regular basis that could be recycled to provide fertiliser for plants. Can you think what it might be?

From *Draw Your Own Encyclopaedia Space Exploration* by Colin M. Drysdale

Is It Possible To Travel To Another Star System?

While it would take about six months to get to Mars, it would take far longer to get to Proxima Centauri, our nearest neighbouring star system. The fastest spacecraft built so far was Helios 2, which reached a speed of 240,000 kilometres an hour. At this speed, it would take 19,000 years to cover the 4.3 light years (the distance light travels in a year) needed to reach Proxima Centauri. This would be over 600 human generations. This means if you left for Proxima Centauri today, it would be your great, great, great (and then 595 more greats) grandchildren that would get there. Do you think this would be possible?

Questions To Answer:

1. What is our nearest neighbouring star system?

2. How far away is it?

3. How long would it take to reach it?

A spacecraft capable of travelling to another star system would need to be big enough for many, many generations of humans to survive on it. If you were in charge of designing such a spaceship, what would it look like? Draw a picture of your idea here.

Quick Fact: An interstellar spaceship would need to house at least one thousand people for many generations. This means it would have to have schools, places to live, places to exercise, places to eat and places for people to work. It would also need places to grow food. This means it would probably feel more like a small town than a spaceship!

How Can We Learn About Other Star Systems?

While it would take tens of thousands of years to travel to other star systems, we can still study and explore them using specially designed scientific instruments. Using them, we can watch stars being born, and dying. We can detect distant planets, and tell if they are suitable for life or if they are just floating in the darkness of interstellar space. We can see galaxies colliding and watch the black hole at the centre of our Milky Way galaxy gobbling up entire star systems. We can even look back in time and see what the universe was like when the very first stars bust into life around fourteen billion years ago.

Questions To Answer:

1. How can we study and explore star systems that are too far away to visit?

2. What type of object is at the centre of the Milky Way?

3. When did the very first stars burst into life?

The Hubble Space Telescope (HST) was launched in 1990. Some of the most amazing photographs it has sent back to Earth are of supernovae. These are exploding stars that send out huge clouds of debris at speeds of over one hundred million kilometres an hour! Find a picture of a supernova taken by the HST and draw a copy of it here. Write the supernova's name below it.

Quick Fact: Most of the chemical elements we find on Earth were first created in supernovae that exploded a very long time ago. This includes all the carbon in our bodies. This means that we are all, quite literally, made of star dust!

What Do You Need To Do To Become A Space Explorer?

There are several ways that you can become a space explorer. The most obvious way is to become an astronaut. To become an astronaut, you first need to get a degree in engineering, biology, physics or maths. You then need to be accepted by a space agency, and successfully complete a strenuous training program that will test your physical and mental fitness. Only a very small number of people who apply ever get to actually go into space. However, you can also become a space explorer without ever leaving planet Earth. You can do this by becoming a scientist and using scientific instruments, like telescopes, to study space.

If you could go anywhere in the Universe, where would you like to go, and what would you like to see? Write your answer down here.

While only trained astronauts get to go into outer space, there is a growing space tourism industry that will fly anyone who can afford it to the very edge of space. What do you think this would feel like? Draw a picture of yourself floating in a spacecraft at the edge of space, and looking back at Earth out of its window.

Quick Fact: Not all space exploration is carried out by scientists and astronauts. There are many citizen science projects that you can take part in without the need for any special training at all. This includes looking for distant planets, searching for asteroids, detecting supernovae and looking for traces of life in other places in the universe! You can find out about projects you can take part in at www.zooniverse.org/projects.

Pop Quiz

The answers to all these questions can be found elsewhere in this book. See if you can answer them all!

1. Who was the first person ever to visit space?
2. How fast do rockets need to go to reach space?
3. What is a space probe?
4. When did the first person walk on the moon?
5. How long did it take the Galileo space probe to reach Jupiter?
6. What is the furthest distance any spacecraft has travelled from Earth?
7. How far did the Opportunity rover travel on Mars during its fourteen year lifespan?
8. When did people first start living on the International Space Station?
9. Where could colonists on Mars get water from?
10. How many generations would it take people to reach Proxima Centauri?
11. What is at the centre of the Milky Way galaxy?
12. When did the first stars burst into life?
13. What type of degree would you need to get to become an astronaut?
14. How many moving parts does a rocket engine have?
15. What was the name of Uri Gagarin's space capsule?
16. How many sunrises do people on the International Space Station see each day?

Write Your Answers Here:

1. _____
2. _____
3. _____
4. _____
5. _____
6. _____
7. _____
8. _____
9. _____
10. _____
11. _____
12. _____
13. _____
14. _____
15. _____
16. _____

Pop Quiz – The Answers

1. The first person ever to visit space was a Russian cosmonaut called Uri Gagarin. He did so on the 12th of April 1961.
2. A rocket needs to travel at more than 40,000 kilometres an hour to overcome Earth's gravity and reach space.
3. A space probe is an unmanned spacecraft filled with cameras and other scientific instruments used to study planets and other objects in our solar system.
4. The first person to walk on the moon was Neil Armstrong. He did so in 1969.
5. The Galileo space probe was launched in October 1989, but it didn't reach Jupiter, its intended destination, for another six years and two months.
6. The furthest distance any spacecraft has travelled is over twenty billion kilometres.
7. The Opportunity rover travelled more than forty-five kilometres across the surface of Mars in its fourteen year life time.
8. The first people started living on the International Space Station in the year 2000, and since then there has always been a crew of between three and six people on board.
9. Colonists on Mars could get water by melting ice that can be found buried below the Martian surface. They could use electricity from solar panels to provide the energy to do this.
10. Travelling at the speed of the fastest spacecraft built to date (Helios 2), it would take over 600 human generations to cover the 4.3 light years needed to reach Proxima Centauri.
11. At the centre of the Milky Way galaxy is a massive black hole capable of gobbling up entire star systems. While our solar system is in this galaxy, it is a very long way from the centre of it, so it isn't in any danger.
12. The first stars burst into life around fourteen billion years ago.
13. In order to become an astronaut, you'd need to get a degree in engineering, maths, physics or biology.
14. Rocket engines have no moving parts what-so-ever!
15. Uri Gagarin's space capsule was called Vostock 1.
16. The International Space Station circles the Earth every 92 minutes, meaning that the people living on it get to see fifteen sunrises every day.

From *Draw Your Own Encyclopaedia Space Exploration* by Colin M. Drysdale

Where To Find Out More About Space Exploration

If you would like to brush up on your knowledge of space exploration, you can check out the following resources:

- **Wikipedia:** *en.wikipedia.org/wiki/Space_exploration.*
- **Encyclopaedia Britannica:** *www.britannica.com/science/space-exploration.*
- **List of Solar System Probes:** This article provides a list of all the probes we have sent to other places in our solar system. You can find it at *en.wikipedia.org/wiki/List_of_Solar_System_Probes.*

Online Content About Space Exploration That You Can Share With Your Class

Below is a list of free online content about space exploration which is suitable for primary-age children that you can share with your students:

- **Escape Velocity – A Quick History Of Space Exploration:** Running time - 4 mins 23 secs. *https://youtu.be/PLcE3AI9wwE.*
- **Voyager – Humanity's Furthest Journey:** Running time - 3 mins 9 secs. *https://youtu.be/PLcE3AI9wwE.*
- **Mars Rovers – A National Geographic Video:** Running time - 3 mins 12 secs. *https://video.nationalgeographic.com/video/00000144-0a2b-d3cb-a96c-7b2f6a460000.*
- **What Is Life Like On The International Space Station?** Running time - 2 mins 37 secs. *https://youtu.be/LkvsWBfmgtw.*
- **Welcome To Mars:** Running time - 4 mins 56 secs. *https://youtu.be/9I7HFpkYB9M.*
- **The Future Of Human Space Exploration:** Running time - 10 mins 52 secs. *https://youtu.be/Zsf4NXcE4Qg.*
- **Hubble Space Telescope – A National Geographic Video:** Running time - 2 mins 44 secs. *https://video.nationalgeographic.com/video/00000144-0a2c-d3cb-a96c-7b2dc5ad0000.*
- **Images From The Hubble Space Telescope:** This site provides an archive of the best pictures of distant objects in space taken by the Hubble Space Telescope. *www.spacetelescope.org/Images/archive/top100/.*

Ideas For Additional Classroom Activities

These additional classroom activities will help make learning about space exploration for your students more fun:

1. **Create A Timeline Of The History Of Space Exploration:** The first human object was sent into space in 1957, and since then we have been exploring it using many different spacecraft. For this activity, start by creating a timeline that covers the period from 1957 until the present day. Add on to it significant technological and social moments for context (like the invention of the first personal computer, the invention of the internet, the launch of the world wide web, Google, Facebook, and the first cell phone). Now, divide your class into pairs and assign each pair a specific spacecraft. They then have to write a short fact file about that spacecraft outlining when it was launched, what it was designed to do, where it went and how long its mission lasted. Next, ask them to draw a picture of their spacecraft, and add both it and their fact file to the space exploration timeline. This will give them a greater understanding of how space exploration has changed over time.

2. **Design A Martian Space Colony:** Set your students the task of designing a colony where people could live on Mars. Divide them into groups, and ask each group to design a specific element of it. These can include where the people would live, where they would work, where and how they would get their power, where they would get water from, how they would grow their food, how they would communicate with people back on Earth. Once they have settled on their design, ask each group to create a drawing or a model of their particular element, and explain to the rest of the class how it would work and why they chose their specific design. Finally, then bring them all together to create your very own Martian space colony.

3. **Play Spacecraft Higher-or-Lower:** Using the characteristics of different spacecraft in the tables at the back of this book, you can play a game of Higher-or-Lower. To do this, first put the names of all the spacecraft into a hat, and draw one out at random. Select a category (such as the year it was launched, how far it travelled or how big it was) and tell your students what the value is for the selected spacecraft. Now draw the name of a second spacecraft out of the hat, and ask your students to tell you if the value for that spacecraft is higher or lower than the value for the first one. If they are right, they win that spacecraft. Repeat this process until all the names have been drawn from the hat, and then count up how many spacecraft they have won off you. Is it more or less than the number you still hold? This game can also be played with the fact file cards created in the first additional classroom.

4. **Create Your Own Voyager-style Disc:** Each of the Voyager spacecraft launched in 1977 carries a golden record disc containing information that will tell any aliens who find it where Earth is and what life here is like. You can find out what was on this disc at *en.wikipedia.org/wiki/Contents_of_the_Voyager_Golden_Record*. Discuss this list of items with your class and then ask them to come up with a list of items that they would put on such a disc to tell aliens all about their lives in 21st Century Earth.

5. **Take Part In A Citizen Science Space Project:** Why just teach your class about space exploration when you can help them become real-life space explorers? To do this, all you need to do is find a suitable citizen science space project and then help them take part. You can find a list of current projects that you can potentially help your class take part in at *www.zooniverse.org/projects?discipline=astronomy&page=1&status=live*.

6. **Build An Air-powered Bottle Rocket:** This is a great experiment to help you students understand how a rocket engine can work without any moving parts. It requires that you purchase a bottle-rocket kit, such as the Rokit Bottle Rocket Kit (available from *www.amazon.co.uk/ROKIT-Bottle-Rocket-Pressure-Action/dp/B001MW7S1E/*). This kit contains a rocket engine that you can attach to a plastic water bottle, and with the aid of a foot pump, you can use it to demonstrate how a rocket engine works. In addition, you can explore how to design a rocket by using different shapes and sizes of bottles to see what effect this has on the distance that they travel. Similarly, you can vary the amount of water that you add to them to see what impact this has on the rocket's performance.

Handouts And Additional Information

On the following pages, you will find a variety of handouts and additional information that you can use during additional classroom activities to accompany the information provided in this book.

1. **Blank *Draw Your Own Encyclopaedia* Pages:** Ask you students to pick a spacecraft, or another aspect of space exploration, and get them to create their own pair of *Draw Your Own Encyclopaedia* pages about it using these blank templates. Once they are finished, bring them all together to create your classes very own custom *Draw Your Own Encyclopaedia* all about human space exploration.

2. **How Much Food Would People Need To Grow To Support A Colony On Mars?** This handout provides all the information your students need to work out how much food a colony of ten people would need to grow each year to get enough food to eat.

3. **How Long Would It Take A Spacecraft To Reach The Other Planets In Our Solar System?** This handout provides all the information your students need to work out how long it would take a spacecraft to reach the other planets in our solar system.

4. **Information About The Characteristics Of Different Spacecraft:** This section provides information about the characteristics of a range of different spacecraft that you can use during the additional classroom activities suggested to accompany this book.

Quick Fact:

Questions To Answer:

Quick Fact:

How Much Food Would People Need To Grow To Support A Colony On Mars?

It would be too expensive and complicated to send regular shipments of food to Mars to support a colony there. This means that the only way we could establish a colony on Mars would be if it could grow enough food to feed all the colonists that live there. Many plants we grow for food on Earth couldn't grow on Mars, but there is one plant that would grow very well in Martian soil. This is the potato, but could a Martian colony grow enough potatoes to feed all its colonists? Once we have a few basic facts, we can use maths to work this out.

One kilogram of potatoes contains 770 calories. This means that the average adult human who has a physically demanding lifestyle (like living on Mars) would need to eat 4 kilograms of potatoes each day. A single potato plant will give a crop of 2.5 kilograms of potatoes per year. From this information, we can work out how many potato plants a Martian colony would need to grow each year to support one colonist. This is done by multiplying the number of potatoes that they would need to eat each day (4 kilograms) by the number of days in a year (365 days), and then dividing the answer by the weight of potatoes that each potato plant will give you each year (2.5 kilograms). How many potato plants would a Mars colony need to grow each year to support a single person?

_____ potato plants.

How many potato plants would they need to grow each year to support a colony of ten people?

_____ potato plants.

Each potato plant would need 0.85 m² to grow. From this information, you can work out how big an area this Martian colony would need to farm to grow enough potatoes to support its ten members. See if you can work this out and write your answer below.

A Martian colony would need to farm an area of _____ m² to grow enough potatoes each year to support them.

To help you visualise how big an area this is, you can compare it to the area of something you are familiar with, like the area of a football pitch. Give that a standard football pitch is typically 100m long and 50m wide, how does its area compare the area needed to grow enough potatoes to support a Martian colony of ten people?

From *Draw Your Own Encyclopaedia Space Exploration* by Colin M. Drysdale

How Long Would It Take A Spacecraft To Reach The Other Planets In Our Solar System?

When planning any space mission, it is important to know how long it will take your spacecraft to reach its destination. This is particularly true for crewed missions, where you need to make sure that there is enough food, water and oxygen onboard for everyone to survive the trip. We can work out how long it will take a spacecraft to travel from Earth to another planet by dividing the distance to the planet by the speed of the spacecraft.

For example, the shortest distance between Earth and Mars is 54.6 million kilometres (54,600,000 km). If a spacecraft travels at 20,000 kilometres an hour, we can work out how long it would take to get to Mars by dividing the distance (54,600,000) by this speed (20,000). This gives an answer of 2,730 hours. If this number is divided by 24 (the number of hours in a day), you can work out how many days this is, and it is 113.75 days.

Given the shortest distances between the Earth and the other planets in our solar system provided in the table below, work out how many days it would take a spacecraft travelling at 20,000 kilometres an hour to reach it.

Planet	Shortest Distance From Earth (km)	The Number Of Days It Would Take A Spacecraft To Get There
Mercury	77,000,000	
Venus	38,000,000	
Mars	54,600,000	113.75 days
Jupiter	588,000,000	
Saturn	1,200,000,000	
Uranus	1,600,000,000	
Neptune	4,300,000,000	

From *Draw Your Own Encyclopaedia Space Exploration* by Colin M. Drysdale

Table Of Characteristics Of Different Spacecraft Used In Space Exploration.

Created to provide additional classroom activities to accompany *Draw Your Own Encyclopaedia Space Exploration* by Colin M. Drysdale (ISBN: 978-10909832-49-7)

Name	Date Launched	Length of Mission	Size	Speed	Longest Distance From Earth	Crewed or Not?	Notable Fact About Its Mission
Sputnik 1	4 October 1957	21 days	83.6 kg	29,000 km/h	939 km	No	First man-made object in space. Its batteries died after 21 days, but it continued to orbit the Earth for a further two months.
Vostok 1	12 April 1961	1 hour 48 minutes	4,725 kg	~39,000 km/h	327 km	Yes (1)	Vostok 1 was the first ever crewed space mission.
Apollo 11	16 July 1969	8 days, 3 hours	45,702 kg	39,897 km/h	384,000 km	Yes (3)	Apollo 11 was the first mission to land people on the moon.
Voyager I	5 September 1977	42 years (so far)	826 kg	62,140 km/h	21.5 billion km (so far)	No	Voyager I has travelled further than any other spacecraft. It crossed into interstellar space in 2013.
Voyager II	20 August 1977	42 years (so far)	826 kg	55,230 km/h	18 billion km (so far)	No	Voyager II is the only spacecraft to have visited Uranus and Neptune. It crossed into interstellar space in 2018.
Space Shuttle Columbia	12 April 1981	2 days 6 hours	2,030,000 kg	28,200 km/h	274 km	Yes (2)	The Space Shuttle Columbia was the first re-usable space craft ever launched.
Galileo	18 October 1989	14 years	2,563 kg	172,800 km/h	968,000,000 km	No	Galileo was the first spacecraft to orbit Jupiter, allowing us to study it in great detail.
Mars Pathfinder	4 December 1996	9 months 23 days	890 kg	26,460 km/h	401,000,000 kilometres	No	This was the first spacecraft successfully land a robotic rover (called Sojourner) on another planet.
Hubble Space Telescope	24 April 1990	29 years (so far)	11,110 kg	28,620 km/h	540 km	No	The HST is the longest-serving and most successful space telescope launched to date.

Downloaded from *PictishBeastPublications.com*.

Name	Date Launched	Length of Mission	Size	Speed	Longest Distance From Earth	Crewed or Not?	Notable Fact About Its Mission
Cassini-Huygens	15 October 1997	19 years 335 days	5,712 kg	158,400 km/h	1.275 billion km	No	This was the first spacecraft to orbit Saturn and study it in detail. This included landing a probe on Titan, one of its moons.
International Space Station	20 November 1998	21 years (so far)	419,725 kg	27,576 km/h	408 km	Yes (3 - 6)	The International Space Station (ISS) has been occupied continuously since the year 2000
Helios 2	15 January 1976	3 years 5 months	374 kg	240,000 km/h	105,000,000 km	No	Helios 2 (also known as Helios B) is the fastest spacecraft launched to date, and has flown closer to the Sun than any other spacecraft.
Mars Global Surveyor	7 November 1996	9 years 11 months	1,030 kg	16,920 km/h	401,000,000 km	No	This was the first spacecraft to study all aspects of Mars in great detail.
Near Shoemaker	17 February 1996	5 years 21 days	800 kg	50,000 km/h (estimated)	330,000,000 km	No	This was the first spacecraft to orbit and land on an asteroid (called Eros).
Salyut 1	19 April 1971	175 days (occupied for 24 days)	18,425 kg	27,000 km/h (estimated)	222 km	Yes (3)	This was the first space station, which allowed people to stay in space for a long period of time, ever launched into space.
Mariner 9	30 May 1971	1 year 150 days	997.9 kg	26,966 km/h	401,000,000 km	No	Mariner 9 was the first spacecraft to orbit another planet (in this case Mars).
Opportunity Mars Rover	7 July 2003 2011	14 years	185 kg	0.18 km/h (on Mars).	401,000,000 km	No	Opportunity's mission was meant to last for ninety days, but it ended up lasting 14 years!
Rosetta	2 March 2004	12 years 6 months	2,900 kg	55,000 km/h	1 billion km	No	This was the first spacecraft to orbit a comet and land a probe (called Philae) on it.
New Horizons	19 January 2006	13 years (so far)	478 kg	58,500 km/h	3.26 billion km	No	When New Horizon set off to study Pluto it was still classified as a planet. By the time the spacecraft got there, Pluto had been demoted to a dwarf planet.

Books available now in the *Draw Your Own Encyclopaedia* series from Pictish Beast Publications:

1. **Mammals** - ISBN: 978-1-909832-39-8. RRP: UK: £6.99 US: $8.99.
2. **Birds** - ISBN: 978-1-909832-41-1. RRP: UK: £6.99 US: $8.99.
3. **Reptiles** - ISBN: 978-1-909832-42-8. RRP: UK: £6.99 US: $8.99.
4. **Amphibians** - ISBN: 978-1-909832-43-5. RRP: UK: £6.99 US: $8.99.
5. **Fish** - ISBN: 978-1-909832-44-2. RRP: UK: £6.99 US: $8.99.
6. **Invertebrates** - ISBN: 978-1-909832-45-9. RRP: UK: £6.99 US: $8.99.
7. **Animals Box Set** – ISBN: 978-1-909832-51-0. RRP: UK: £39.99 US:$49.99.
8. **Scotland's Dolphins** - ISBN: 978-1-909832-55-8. RRP: UK: £6.99 US: $8.99.
9. **Scotland's Seabirds** - ISBN: 978-1-909832-59-6. RRP: UK: £6.99 US: $8.99.
10. **Scotland's Native Wildlife** - ISBN: 978-1-909832-59-6. RRP: UK: £6.99 US: $8.99.
11. **Scotland's Castles** - ISBN: 978-1-909832-62-6. RRP: UK: £6.99 US: $8.99.
12. **Scotland's Folklore** - ISBN: 978-1-909832-63-3. RRP: UK: £6.99 US: $8.99.
13. **Our Solar System** - ISBN: 978-1-909832-46-6. RRP: UK: £6.99 US: $8.99.
14. **Space Exploration** - ISBN: 978-1-909832-49-7. RRP: UK: £6.99 US: $8.99.

Books coming soon in the *Draw Your Own Encyclopaedia* series:

1. **Planet Earth** - ISBN: 978-1-909832-50-3. RRP: UK: £6.99 US: $8.99.
2. **Deep Space** - ISBN: 978-1-909832-47-3. RRP: UK: £6.99 US: $8.99.
3. **The Universe** - ISBN: 978-1-909832-48-0. RRP: UK: £6.99 US: $8.99.

For more information on this series of books (including a full list of available and upcoming titles), visit: *www.pictishbeastpublications.com/draw-your-own-encyclopaedia*

www.ingramcontent.com/pod-product-compliance
Lightning Source LLC
Chambersburg PA
CBHW050716090526
44587CB00019B/3405